MY DAD CAN DO ANYTHING!

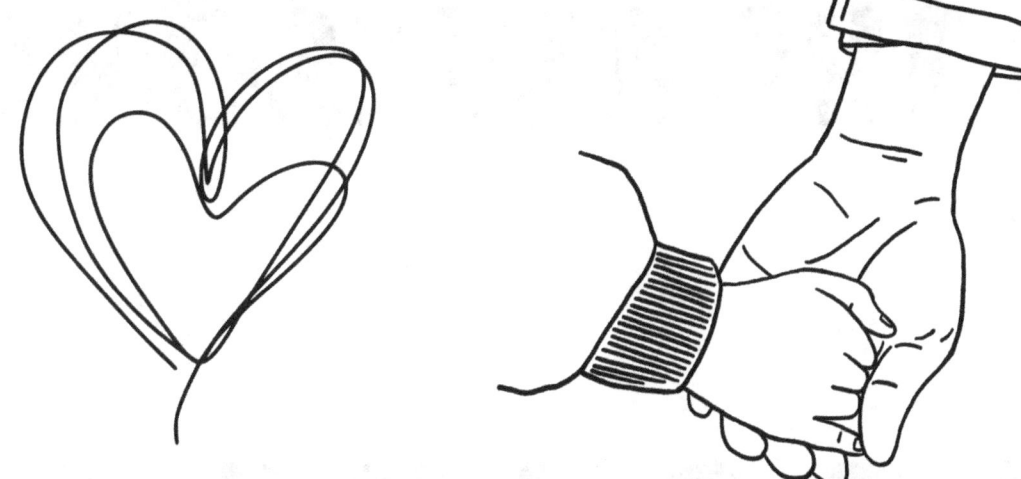

A Father's day coloring book for kids to color showcasing the various jobs Dads do to provide for their family

By Stephanie Katz

THIS BOOK BELONGS TO THE AWESOME:

• • • • • • • • • •

Copyright 2023 by Stephanie Katz ©
All Rights Reserved. No Parts of this book may be distributed
or reproduced or transmitted in any way shape or form
Without the Author's Written and Signed Permission.

My father is my Superhero

My Dad is a pilot,
He transports people from one country to another

My father is my

My Dad is a pilot,
He flies around
the world.

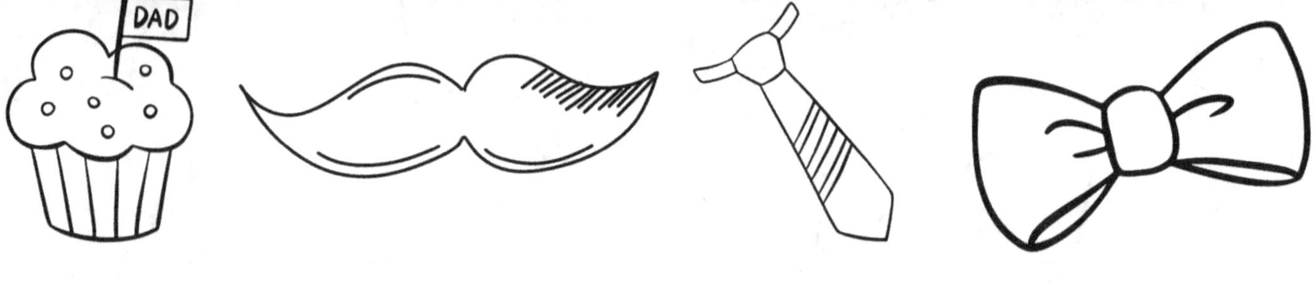

Superhero

My father is my Superhero

My Dad is an astronaut,
He travels through space

My father is my Superhero

My Dad is an astronaut,
He discovers new planets.

My father is my Superhero

My Dad is an astronaut,
He is far from earth
but close in my heart.

My father is my

My Dad is a chef,
he cooks delicious food.

Superhero

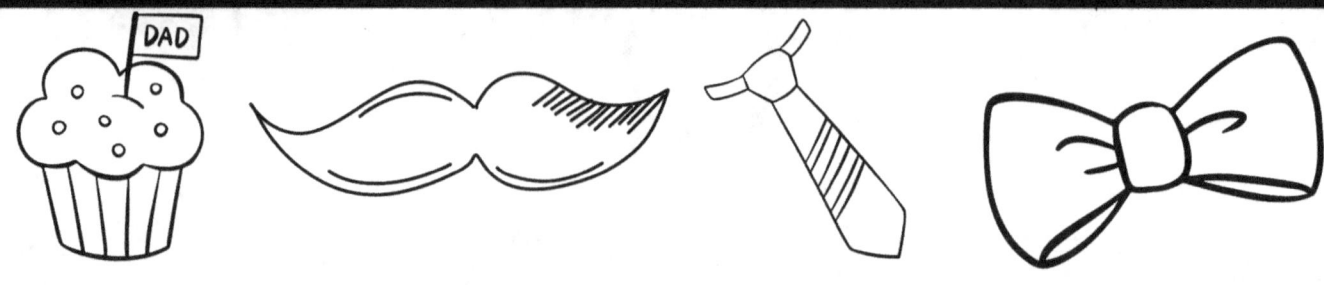

My father is my Superhero

My Dad is a chef,
he makes people happy
by serving them
great meals.

My father is my Superhero

My Dad is a chef but even if he wasn't I would still love his food.

My father is my

My Dad is a teacher, he educates people.

Superhero

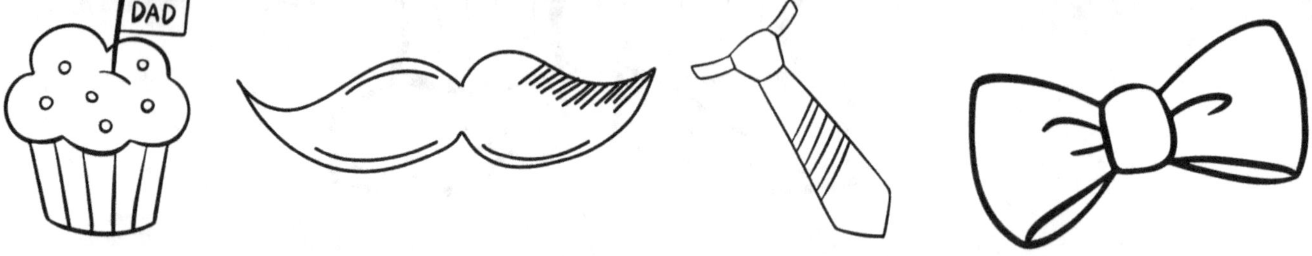

My father is my

My Dad is a teacher, he teaches children about good and evil.

Superhero

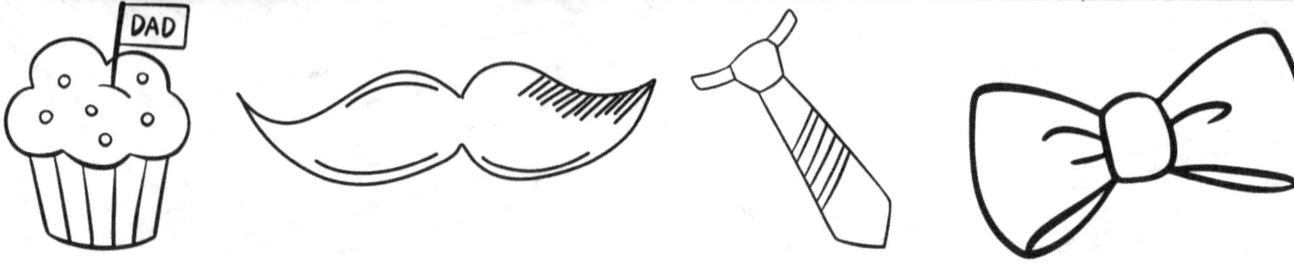

My father is my Superhero

My Dad is a teacher, he likes to share his knowledge.

My father is my Superhero

My Dad is a firefighter, he saves people from flames.

My father is my Superhero

My Dad is a firefighter, he risks his life for others.

My father is my Superhero

My Dad is a firefighter, he protects people.

My father is my Superhero

My Dad is a police officer, he protects people.

My father is my Superhero

My Dad is a police officer, he makes sure people obey the law.

My father is my Superhero

My Dad is a police officer, and he catches criminals and puts them in jail.

My father is my Superhero

My Dad is a doctor, he makes sure people are healthy.

My father is my Superhero

My Dad is a doctor, he makes sure people are never sick.

My father is my Superhero

My Dad is a doctor, he makes sick people feel better.

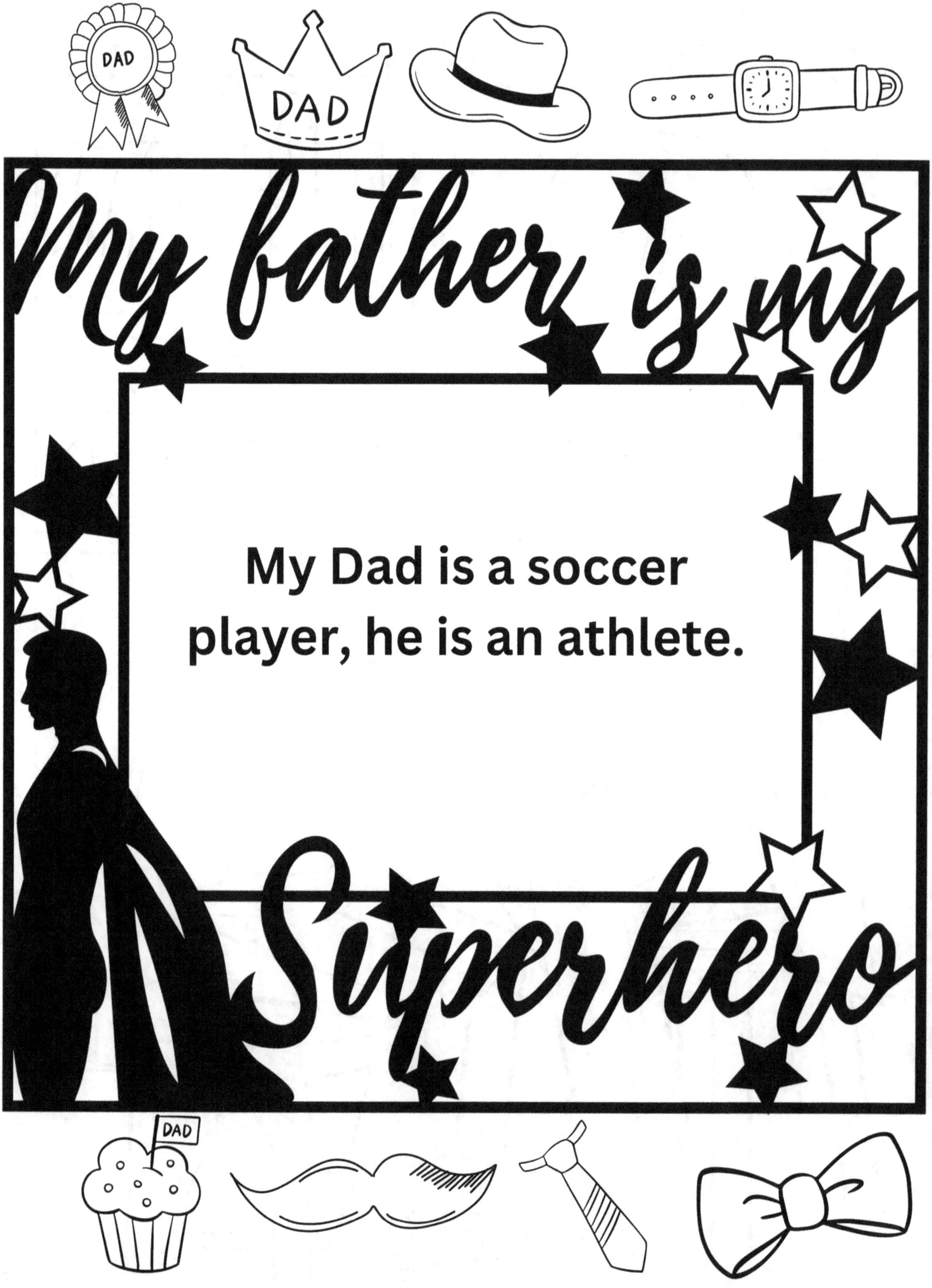
DAD
DAD
My father is my
My Dad is a soccer player, he is an athlete.
Superhero
DAD

My father is my Superhero

My Dad is a soccer player, he entertains crowds with his talent.

My father is my Superhero

My Dad is a soccer player, he knows how to juggle.

My father is my Superhero

My Dad is a scientist,
He discovers new things
about the world.

My father is my Superhero

My Dad is a scientist, his discoveries are important.

My father is my Superhero

My Dad is a scientist, he is wise.

My father is my Superhero

My Dad is a farmer, he plants fruits and vegetables.

My father is my Superhero

My Dad is a farmer, he raises cows, sheeps and pigs.

My father is my Superhero

My Dad is a farmer, he knows the importance of nature and respects it.

My father is my Superhero

Dads all around the world work hard at various jobs to provide for their family. Make sure you tell your dad how much you love him!

www.ingramcontent.com/pod-product-compliance
Lightning Source LLC
Chambersburg PA
CBHW081756100526

44592CB00015B/2457